Find & Fuel Your

Purpose

Charlana Kelly

Author of "You Are Not Here by Accident"
and "Irrefutable."

Find & Fuel Your Purpose

© 2018 by Charlana Kelly.
All Rights Reserved.

No part of this book may be reproduced, stored in a retrieval system, or transmitted
By any means without the written permission of the author and publisher.

Unless otherwise indicated, all Scripture quotations are taken from the Holy Bible, New Living Translation, copyright © 1996, 2004, 2007 by Tyndale House Foundation. Used by permission of Tyndale House Publishers, Inc., Carol Stream, Illinois 60188. All rights reserved.

Italicized references of Scriptures are the author's paraphrase or emphasis as noted.

Published by:

www.speaktruthmedia.com

ISBN: 13: 978-0-9985190-3-6 *(pb)*
ISBN: 13: 978-1-7342646-5-4 *(eb)*

First Printing: 2018 USA
Second printing: 2020 USA

DEDICATION

To YOU, who are called to display and bring glory to your magnificent Creator and Father, the God of ALL the Universe. YOU are His workmanship, His very own chosen vessel. YOU are unique, beautiful, and amazing to behold.

It's YOUR time, because it's His time and He chose to work through His creation, YOU. As you find your purpose in this season, may you be fueled daily to grow more and more like Christ.

No limits, take the limits off right now. We **remove** every **hindrance**, every **obstacle**, every **block** until you are *completely restored* mentally, physically, and spiritually to perfect soundness.

CONTENTS

PURPOSE – The What!

Transformation is His Jam ... 8

A Masterpiece for the Ages ... 10

One Two Five & On & On ... 13

YOU Posses the BEST Gift ... 15

Resist! The Purpose Killers ... 16

PASSION – The How!

Clarity & Consistency ... 19

More Than Life Itself ... 19

The Fire that Ignites the Fuel ... 20

Easily Entreated ... 22

Found in Desire ... 24

PATTERNS – The Where!

Patterns that Produce ... 28

Influence that Shifts ... 30

Beyond the Border ... 32

Entering the Arena ... 33

Forward, ho! ... 35

What's Next ... 38

Chapter One

PURPOSE

*What you are created for,
the reason you exist.*

Contrary to what many people think, every person has a God-given purpose, which is perfectly planned for you. Your spirit was not randomly sent into your body. God chose YOU, decided on the day of your birth and sent you with highly deliberate intention. So, how do you find your purpose? I'm glad you asked! Let's do this together, let's discover "**The What**," what purpose is.

There are two types of PURPOSE that I refer to as "Universal and Unique," the transformation and the beautiful creation.

Transformation is His Jam!

What do I mean by "universal"? It is the same for *all* BELIEVERS. We are all purposed to be transformed into the image of Christ.

Paul beautifully described it to the Romans;

*God knew his people **in advance**, and he **chose** them **to become like his Son*** *(8:29).*

Then, Paul revealed our universal purpose to the Church at Corinth;

*The Lord **makes us** more and more **like him as we are changed into his glorious image*** *(2 Cor. 3:18).*

The key to fulfillment of your universal purpose is daily surrender! No way around it friend, you must give yourself to Him!

It's your reasonable service to offer yourself to God as a living sacrifice and do it in a way that it is wholly acceptable to Him (Romans 12:1—2). Yes!!! Doesn't feel good at first because we always want our way. RIGHT? Nevertheless, it should be our daily pursuit as our reasonable service to the Lord. Trust me, He will be well pleased and you will be transformed. And, He loves transformation, as they say, "It's His jam!"

Remember surrender? It looks like this. Every opportunity you have to act like and look like Jesus in your words and actions, you take it willingly and joyfully. Keep being like Jesus to everyone around you and you will live in an overflow of joy!

Trust me I know how many opportunities we have daily, whether interacting with our family members, in traffic, on the job, or in the marketplace, opportunities to surrender to Jesus' way of doing and being are innumerable.

Look for ways to bless people and prefer others over yourself. This is surrender and it never ends, but it's transformation will become who you are without having to decide every time an opportunity presents itself.

A Masterpiece for the Ages

Remember the second type of purpose? Unique, which is displayed through your God-given talent. It's the real you, the spiritual you, the perfect you, the one-of-a-kind you. I love something Max Lucado once wrote, "God made you and He broke the mold." He was absolutely right!

First things first, do you know what your gifts and talents are? In Scripture, "gifts" are a manifestation of the Spirit that empowers us to do something in the name of God through grace or endowment. "Talents," on the other hand, have a monetary value. In the world, talents could be singing, dancing, speaking, or a myriad of other special activities that we are gifted at above others.

These are unique to each person and continue to increase as we prove ourselves faithful with each. They are given to us so that we can use them to bring glory to God. Paul wrote about God's gifts to the Romans:

__We have different gifts__, according to the grace given to each of us. If your gift is prophesying, then prophesy in accordance with your faith; if it is __serving, then serve__; if it is __teaching, then teach__; if it is to __encourage, then give encouragement__; if it is __giving, then give generously__; if it is to __lead, do it diligently__; if it is to show mercy, do it cheerfully (12:6—8).

It's a good time to discover your gifts if you don't already know what they are. Do an inventory and write the top three here.

1) _____
2) _____
3) _____

My next question is, "Are you using them"? Perhaps you don't have an opportunity to operate in your gifts or you don't know where to start. Either way, when you use them for God's glory you are fulfilling your purpose. To begin using your unique purpose, consider and answer these questions.

> #1 – How can I use my talents?
> #2 – Where can I use my talents?

Keys to fulfilling your unique purpose are service, obedience, and faithfulness. Make sure you are serving somewhere in the church or community offering your gifts and talent. Look for opportunities, then respond. It all begins in service. Do something with what God gave you!

One Two Five and On and On

We see this so clearly in the Parable of the Talents. Jesus details the reward and increase of faithful servants. Those who did something with the talent entrusted to them heard praise from the master, "well done good and faithful servant, you've been faithful over a few things, I will make you ruler over much" (Matt. 25:23). The Parable is your example of a servant who is faithful with what God has put in his/her hand.

There is absolutely no limit to what God will do with you if you surrender with continued faithfulness and obedience. Your unique purpose will shift and grow, taking you to places you could have never thought possible.

Remember how the servants increased, your unique purpose is progressive. In other words, when you prove yourself faithful with what you hold in your hand, God will give you more and more. No limits at all! You are the only one who can limit your progress and promotion.

I believe the servant given five talents began with one. Why? God never gives us a task too big for us. He asks us to be faithful in least, as we are, we grow in grace and stature becoming able to handle more. I'll use myself as an example here. I didn't start out teaching Bible Studies. I started serving in the Nursery. It was many years before I received an opportunity to teach, but when I started this gift increased too, from small groups to thousands. It all began with one step of obedience and continued faithfulness to bring me to where I am today. And, God's not finished; I'm still being faithful everyday with what is in my hand as I continue to grow.

Your purpose is progressive, but you are in the driver's seat. It's all up to you to determine how far you will go. It's all about growth and that's what God wants. Never give up, keep moving forward.

YOUR Gift is the BEST Gift

Endeavor to learn and grow in your gift. Grace has been given to you to empower your gift. As you become more and more like Jesus, your gift will flourish and grow.

Operate in your gift where you are right now. Be an encourager, serve who and where you can, teach and share with those around you, pray for everyone and take time to worship the Lord.

Paul exhorted the Corinthians to desire the greater gifts. Be hungry for growth and intimate fellowship with the Lord. The greatest of gifts we learn is love, loving God, self, and others. It's the best thing we can give to others. Look every day for ways to love and opportunities to be like Jesus to everyone around you.

Finally, you must learn to resist the behaviors and attitudes that stifle your purpose. Let's consider three.

Resist! The 3 C's that Kill Purpose

Never — ever — compete, compare, or complain. I call these PURPOSE KILLERS. Doing any one of them tells God you don't want what He has blessed you with. Yikes! God forbid you turn down HIS gift.

Any one of these will hold you hostage until you repent, let go, accept, and celebrate your unique purpose in Christ.

God doesn't need another Priscilla Shirer or Christine Cain. We celebrate them, but we are not going to be like them. So, stop desiring to be anyone other than yourself. Trust me you are unique in every way and the whole world is looking for YOU.

Don't feel ashamed or have regret if you have participated in these KILLERS. We are human and it is human nature to want what everybody else has. Even Jesus' disciples had to learn this lesson. They were disputing among themselves to see who should be the greatest. Boy did Jesus knock them down a peg or two or twenty. He told them whoever desired to be first would be last, and servant of all (Mark 9:33—37).

Learn to recognize the earmarks of these purpose killers; jealousy, lording over other people, feelings of being less than, trying to be like someone else. Get alone with your Father and ask Him to search your heart, test and try you, and remove any way in you that hinders your growth in Him and your purpose.

Chapter Two
PASSION

Enthusiastic, obsessed, preoccupied with, fervent, eager, excitement, commitment, dedication, devotion, and joy are just a few adjectives describing passion, which is "**The How**" of purpose. Once you find purpose, you have to put it to practice, use it, fulfill it, and bless the people around you with what God has given you.

Passion does two things; it identifies and fuels or gives power to your purpose. Let me break it down for you.

Clarity & Consistency

Passion clarifies your purpose, creating in you a laser sharp focus. Whatever you focus on sets the course of your life. Once you say, "Yes," to God regarding your purpose, He will open doors, cause paths to cross, make connections for you to use your gifts and fulfill your purpose. Get focused on His plan and you will become clear about your pathway.

Consistency is key to success in every endeavor. If you lack consistency, then it's simple to conclude you lack passion. And, if there's no passion to do something repeatedly, then it's probably not a part of your purpose.

More than Life Itself

You can confirm your purpose through your heart's fervency to fulfill the one thing that brings you joy more than anything else in your life. Love marks your purpose. You will love your purpose more than life itself.

You will work eight hours and burn with desire to get to that place where you go to fulfill your purpose. Whether it's writing, speaking, serving in the community or church, it's not drudgery to you. It's the place where you light up for Jesus!

The Fire that Ignites the Fuel

Your purpose will be fiery, because of your fervency. Passion is the fuel that ignites the fire. Where there's fuel, a spark of "Yes to purpose!" will set you on fire!

Your purpose is NOT something you choose, it's God-given so He has placed the fuel on the inside of you. And, He's given you help to bring it to pass.

Purpose and passion always involve Christ and people. First, think of Christ.

Perhaps you've never known that Jesus' suffering and crucifixion are referred to as "The Passion." Why? Well, let's consider. What an amazing example of purpose. Christ's purpose was the redemption of mankind. He did it by laying His life down for us. He died because He first loved, and the Father loved us so much that He sent His only begotten son to bring us abundant life.

The same is true of your passion. That thing you love more than life itself. Let me ask you a question based on the same purpose Christ fulfilled. Who is it that *you* desire to bring life and reconciliation to? Who are you willing to lay your life down for, so that they can have a better life? These are questions that reveal the depths of your passion.

One thing is for sure, you will not have the passion to fulfill your UNIQUE PURPOSE until you love others more than yourself. The key to passion — selfless love. Do you run from people or to them? When God moves on your heart to do something for someone else, do you do it? Our response time is a real indication of our maturity in Christ. Passionate people respond quickly!

Easily Entreated

As you step out to fulfill your purpose you will find that God trusts you more and more with people. The key to building trust is responding.

When people sense something in the Spirit, they often question whether it is God or not. I understand because I've been there. I had to grow in the knowledge of God to comprehend when He was moving upon me for something or someone.

When you begin to recognize God's ways, you will immediately notice His prompting within your heart or belly. Your only requirement is to respond. I love the way the young prophet-in-training, Samuel, Hannah's son learned to hear and respond to the voice of God. She dedicated him to the Lord's service and brought him to the Temple to be raised by the Prophet Eli. One evening, Samuel heard a voice three times, thinking it was Eli, he went to him. Finally, Eli recognized that Samuel was hearing God's voice. He instructed him how to respond and I love Samuel's words.

The next time Samuel heard God's voice, he responded, "Speak Lord, for Your servant is listening!" Beautiful! Yes, the boy was saying, "Here I am Father, ready, willing, able, and listening. Instruct me, and I will go and do." Of course, that's my paraphrase, but, in essence, it is exactly what Samuel was saying.

Samuel was easily entreated by God. He heard, he listened, he responded, he did. God desires the same of us as we walk out our purpose. You see it's not about us, it's about Him and others.

Psalm 37:4 is one of my favorite Scriptures, there's a word in the verse that describes perfectly what God is looking for from us. The word? **Delight**! In the Hebrew it means, "**soft and pliable, easily entreated**."

In order to fulfill your purpose, you too will have to sharpen your skills, and be soft and pliable to God's instructions. Don't fret about it now, because you will learn and grow. God gave you a Helper, The Holy Spirit, and He will help you, just like Eli helped Samuel.

Found in Desire

God wants to give you the desires of your heart. What are your desires? Whatever they are, your purpose and passion are found right there.

It's all wrapped up in your heart, purpose, and passion. So, guard your heart, make it precious to the Lord. Don't allow the world to corrupt your deepest desires. Keep them set apart for Him alone.

I have a little saying, "My heart is ever before the Lord." You see, when we make it so with our heart, then we are always ready to hear and respond to Him. We keep out the "yuckiness" of the world and allow only that which is pure, noble, kind, precious, beautiful, etc. into our heart and mind.

You are a precious jewel. And God has BIG plans for you. Walk with Him and inquire of Him often throughout your day. He loves your voice and is happy to hear from you every time you whisper your prayers to Him.

Then, when He says pray for this person, you respond with obedience. When He says, give this to that person, you are happy to comply with His request. In doing so, you are fulfilling God's purpose for your life with great passion for Him and others.

Keep your heart open toward the Lord and decide to obey quickly when He prompts you. Oh, the life of happy obedience, it is a blessed one — a joyful blessed life indeed!

Chapter Three
PATTERNS

Now, "**The Where**!"

It's exciting beyond words to get to this point. I bet you have been chomping at the bit, like a thoroughbred horse in the gate at the racetrack, saying, "Let me out, I'm ready to run." Or, maybe not, perhaps you are apprehensive about it all, unsure, and a little frightened about the future your purpose will lead you into.

Often, we see *the where* before we know *the what* or *the how*. If this happens, people step out before they are ready and get smacked. Why? Because they ran ahead of God without anointing, information, wisdom, strategies, awareness of gifting, etc. It can be a harsh dose of reality that sets us back years before we get the courage to get in there with God again.

It's okay if you've done this already, most of us have, even the Prophet Elijah ran ahead of God and used his gifts for the wrong reason. It cost him. But God's mercy is abundant, and our gifts and callings are never revoked by God. We learn and grow, then dip our toe in the water again.

We are practicing with Him, and friend, that just fine with our Daddy God.

Patterns Produce

One of the best ways to discover *where* your purpose is sending you first is to consider the **patterns** or recurring events in your life! Where they unfolded and the people they unfolded for.

Before I go on, I want to share that patterns reveal two things, those that hinder and those that produce fruit. We can discover a lot about ourselves by looking at those events that seem to happen over and over. Faces and names change but the type of event does not.

You want to discover the patterns to bring wholeness to your life and to release you into the blessing and prosperity God has planned for you through your purpose. Get those hindering patterns healed and stopped, then watch the producing patterns take off with unlimited potential in Christ.

I'll use myself as a quick example here. First the producing pattern. My entire life has had a reoccurring pattern of standing up for what is right in God's eyes and being a voice for the voiceless. On the hindering side, I've always had to deal with "father figures" who do not support me through encouragement and strength. When the going got tough in my life, they were either absent or didn't come to my defense. Whew! When I got the revelation of this and dealt with it to the point of healing, I soared like an eagle.

I digress, my life's pattern has shown up time and time again as I have found myself in a situation where I must speak up. Whether as a kid speaking for her friend who was falsely accused, a Program Director standing up for disadvantaged children who were being denied services, or a minister uncovering lies and false teaching.

The patterns in your life are an indication of *where* God is taking you; what arena or mountain of culture you will ultimately influence with your gifts.

Influence that Shifts

God's plan is always deliverance of

His people and expansion of His kingdom. He uses you and me to fulfill His plan. We need only be faithful and obedient.

You are called to bring **deliverance.** To possess, dispossess, inherit, destroy, occupy, seize, supplant enemy territory. **Expand** and **advance** the kingdom of God: Possess, inherit, occupy in Jesus' name wherever you physically reside. **Pushback** the kingdom of darkness: Dispossess, destroy, seize, supplant the kingdom of darkness.

Sometimes by your presence alone **atmospheres will shift**, light pierces through, healing, deliverance, salvation come in Jesus name.

You must be **AWARE** of God's power moving through you. If you aren't aware of this you will have no impact. If you are, you will enforce impact and witness a heavenly change.

Just remember, your gift should always bring LIFE in Christ's name for God's glory.

So, find your place and serve. Watch the atmosphere shift as you bring heaven to earth.

Purpose all begins with one step by way of an opportunity or invitation that comes.

Beyond the Border

My husband and I were always in the business industry, but when I felt a call to the ministry, as I shared earlier, I started serving right where I was at, grew in grace and was trusted with more. I served in the church, community, government, and legal arenas.

As you serve, you too will grow in grace and God will trust you. All that's required is daily faithfulness where you are right now.

As Jesus told the faithful servants in the Parable of the Talents, "you have been faithful with least, I will make you ruler over much." It begins with one person and increases from there.

That's when borders expand, influence increases, and you go far beyond the place *where* you believe you are purposed to be today.

Don't ever get overtaken by what you perceive about your future, get up each morning, look at what's in your hand, and do something with it.

When you do, you will be amazed by all the miraculous moments God will give you because of your daily acts of obedience.

Entering the Arena

What picture do you get when you think about an arena? Sports? Or, maybe the ancient arenas where gladiators battled? So many examples, right?

When we say "yes" to God's purpose and discover our *where*, that place is the spiritual arena God wants you to impact with heaven, the Gospel, deliverance, healing, restoration, etc. He wants YOU to advance the kingdom of God right there in that arena.

Paul wrote about a "sphere of influence," where God had given him authority and power to preach the Gospel, disciple people, plant churches, etc. We all have a sphere of influence, our family, friends, fellow believers, coworkers, community, and church. Our culture is also broken up into spheres or mountains as some have termed them. Believers should be influencing those places, daily. We aren't called to all seven, most often to several.

These spheres include, family, church, community, business, media, education, government. Your unique purpose will influentially take you into three or more of these arenas. Why three?

We are all called to influence our family, the church, and community. But you might have a passion for children and their education. Therefore, consider how you can influence education with kingdom principles and the Gospel. Use the same principle of thought for the other arenas I included above.

Perhaps today you are focused on your family alone and that's okay. Remember, your purpose is progressive, so expect God to give you more when you prove yourself faithful with your family. I'm a firm believer our call begins in the home! We don't have to have a perfect family, but we do have to have a perfect heart toward our family, desiring God's BEST for each one and being the advocate in prayer for their future.

Forward, ho!

I've always wanted to use that old saying which simply means to urge onward! I'm urging you onward today into the greatest adventure you can ever imagine. I promise you God's plans are best and His purpose for you is immeasurably good, filled with blessing, joy, love, peace, and satisfaction beyond your comprehension.

Is life perfect? No. Will there be challenges? Yes. But, how does it feel to know that the King of the Universe and the Creator of All is in your corner. He fixed the fight, the battle is His, and the victory is won. You need only walk through every opened door, keep your eyes on Jesus, your heart before God, and your determination centered around advancing the kingdom of God on earth.

Take His love and mercy, joy, and peace to the nations. Yes YOU! I'm writing to YOU.

I'll end this mini-book with my absolute, all-time, favorite Scripture in the big Book, Psalm 85:10—13;

> *"Mercy and truth have **met together**; Righteousness and peace **have kissed**.*

Truth shall spring out of the earth, and righteousness shall look down from heaven.

*Yes, the Lord **will give what is good**; And our land will **yield its increase**. Righteousness will go before Him, and shall **make His footsteps our pathway**.*

I hope you can see why these verses are my favorites. The words paint a beautiful picture of what it looks like for us to walk with God. Think about it! We meet, we kiss, God gives what is good, we yield increase of spiritual fruit, He goes before us as a shield, and makes His footsteps our pathway.

These words remind me of something my earthly father use to do. I'd put my feet on top of his and he'd walk me around. It was so much fun, almost like a dance. Are you getting where I'm going? Yes! We do the same thing with our Daddy God. We put our tiny feet on top of His and with all the good and glorious blessing of heaven He walks us around right down the path of His purpose for our life.

Just say "Yes!" And, let's walk the pathway together with Him. I'll cheer you on and listen when you need someone to talk to. No matter what, I say right now, "Forward, ho!"

Let's GO, let's do it for Him and others. Let's fill heaven with beautiful people from every part of the world.

I'm urging you onward. But, know this, I'm in it with you! We are walking together as we progressively fulfill God's glorious purpose for our lives.

What's Next?

Okay, so I dropped a lot on you here. Now, you need a mentor/advocate, a coach in today's vernacular, that will help you along the way. Good news because I have a private Facebook group and a 21-day intensive to help you discover your purpose, empower your passion, recognize your patterns, and launch you out into your mission for Christ.

You can join any time there's open enrollment and go as far as you'd like with me to hold your hand, provide a safe place, with encouraging support that will empower you to go far beyond where you hope to today.

You can connect with me on social media for more information through this handle, @charlanakelly. I look forward to connecting and hearing from you.

Until then, I'm cheering you on to victory in everything you do!

About the Author

Charlana Kelly understands what it is like to have a sense that there's something great God has created you to do. She didn't always have a leader/mentor who believed in her or recognized her gifts and purpose. She understands the agony people can feel as they wait in what seems like perpetuity for someone, anyone to step in with guidance and empowerment.

Over the years, God has given her a passion to come along side of women to help them discover their gifts, purpose, and high calling. She has also made room for them with opportunities to use their gifts in the ministries she has established over the past twenty plus years.

She believes in YOU, and she will walk along side of you to help you discover your gifts, purpose, and calling too, then empower you to become everything God ordained you to be in this strategic hour for the kingdom of God.

Charlana is a multiple times author, speaker, Bible teacher, television host, life coach, business/ministry consultant, and CEO of SpeakTruth Media Group LLC. She's a leader of leaders of leaders who believes you have the potential to impart, empower, create, build, and release leaders into their destiny too.

Virginia born, Florida raised, happy Texas transplant, this sunshine girl speaks truth and inspires many to influence the world around them. She is always encouraging leaders, loving people, sharing Christ, and changing the atmosphere around her.

Invitations & Contact Info

Charlana is currently open for invitations to speak at your church/event and would love to hear from you. She resides in East Texas; however, she will travel within the US and to other nations. She has spoken at churches and conferences both large and small in the United States as well as Haiti, India, Kenya, and Jamaica.

Please contact by email, to initiate an invitation for ministry at your church, conference, event, or workshop. Please include some details, so we can get the scope of the vision you have for your event. Send to: charlana@charlanakelly.org.

Charlana prayerfully considers the times and seasons of the Lord and His plans for His people throughout the earth. She is always honored and blessed to be a part of ministry to and for the Body of Christ. Over the years, she has often been the primary speaker at events, however she loves being part of a team of speakers and enjoys watching God use the dynamics of different ministers to bring salvation, healing, and restoration to His people.

Connect, Learn, Grow, Go

Mail: PO Box 1448, Crockett TX 75835-7448
Email: charlana@charlanakelly.org

Social Media
Instagram – Charlana Kelly
Facebook – Charlana Kelly
Twitter – Charlana Kelly
YouTube – Charlana Kelly TV

Online Courses & Training
The Engage Institute of Discipleship & Leadership
Coming Soon

Other Books by Charlana Kelly
In Search of the King's Court © 2006
Reaching Out with a Message of Hope © 2007
You are Not Here by Accident © 2017
Find & Fuel Your Purpose © 2017
Irrefutable © 2018

Weekly TV Program
ENGAGE for Influence Grace TV
Friday at 7pm & Sunday at 7am
On-demand at @charlanakellyTV

www.ingramcontent.com/pod-product-compliance
Lightning Source LLC
Chambersburg PA
CBHW050449010526
44118CB00013B/1753